Creating Wordpress Online Store and Wordpress Online Magazine

By
Dr. Hidaia Alassouli

a) Abstract:

The objective of this work is to develop a Word Press Online Store with Different Ecommerce Plugins and Themes and Word Press Online Magazine with MH Magazine Theme

The work consists of three parts:

i. Part I: Building Personal Websie with online shop the sell Ebooks:

The objective of this part is to develop a Ecommerce word press website with all commonly used Plug-ins.

First I registered in some free webhost my domain http://hidaia-alassouli.000space.com

Then I created the database and installed the word press package.

I installed after that all important Plugins for my website. I tested different ecommerce plugin to sell ebooks .The report includes:

1- Changing the wordpress theme.
2- Creating the frontpage post and the other pages.
3- Adding Gallery Plugin.
4- Adding yoast.
5- Submission the Site to Search Engine and Analyze your Website
6- Adding Contact Form Plugin
7- Using easyfiledownloads Plugin to sell ebooks
8- Using WP-Ecommerce Plugin to sell ebooks
9- Using WP Shopping Cart Plugin
10- Using Woocommerce Plugin to sell my Ebooks

I ended up to build my ecommerce shop with woocommerce as it was the most efficient and comfortable.

ii. Part II: Building Ecomerce website with mystile theme and woocommerce plugin

The objective of this part is to develop a Ecommerce website with mystyle theme and woocommerce plugin and other commonly used Plug-ins.
First I registered in some free webhost my domain http://hedaya-alasooly.000space.com

Then I created the database and installed the word press package.

I installed after that all important Plugins for my website. The second part of report includes:

1- Installing mystyle theme.
2- Installing woocommerce plugin Plugin.
3- Adding yoast seo Plugin.
4- Submission the Site to Search Engine and Analyze your Website

iii.   **Part III: Building Online magazine website with MH-Magazine theme**

The objective of this part is to develop an online magazine website with MH Magazine theme and other commonly used Plug-ins.

First I registered in some free webhost my domain http://anticorruption.000space.com.

Then I created the database and installed the word press package.

I installed after that all important Plugins for my website. The third part of report includes:

1- Installing MH Magazine theme.
2- Configuring MH Magazine theme.
3- Adding yoast seo Plugin.
4- Submission the Site to Search Engine and Analyze your Website

b) Part I: Building Personal Websie with online shop the sell Ebooks:

i. Registering in Free Web Host and Creating Domain

You can see in the web site http://www.absolutely-free-hosting.com/free_hosts_01.php some of the free web hosting. I chose to install my site in the www.000space.com

I created an account in www.000space.com. I created the subdomain http://hidaia-alassouli.000space.com. The following account details are provided

Main Hosting Details

Control panel username	space_15864003
Control panel password	**********
Control panel URL	**cpanel.000space.com**
MySQL username	space_15864003
MySQL password	**********
MySQL hostname	sql209.000space.com

FTP username	space_15864003
FTP password	**********
FTP host name	ftp.000space.com

Your Website URL's

Home page	http://hidaia-alassouli.000space.com

ii. Creating MySQL database

1. Under database management in control panel, choose MySQL database
2. Create database with a name as example space_15864003_wpress

iii. Downloading and installing wordpress package.

1. Download wordpress 4.1 from http://wordpress.org/download/ site in your desktop.
2. Try to uncompress the zip file, then compress all contents of word press folder in new zip file wordpress.zip
3. In the web hosting control panel under file management, choose online file manager
4. Go to htdocs directory
5. Click upload, then choose to upload Archives (zip, tar, tgz, gz) and upload wordpress.zip.
6. Browse again to /hidaia-alassouli.000space.com/htdocs directory, and there will be file wp-config-sample.php, rename the file in the file manager to wp-config.php, and edit the file in the following points:

   // ** MySQL settings - You can get this info from your web host ** //
   /** The name of the database for WordPress */
   define('DB_NAME', ' space_15864003_wpress');
   /** MySQL database username */
   define('DB_USER', ' space_15864003');
   /** MySQL database password */
   define('DB_PASSWORD', 'main password');
   /** MySQL hostname */
   define('DB_HOST', ' sql209.000space.com ');

7. Now in the internet browser go to the website http://www.hidaia-alassouli.000space.com and continue the installation of the wordpress package. Note you will be required the username and password of the administrator. Even if you did not create the wpconfig.php before, the installation process can create it and will ask you the previous mentioned database information in step 5. To administer wordpress, you need to go to http://www.hidaia-alassouli.000space.com /wp-admin

iv. Changing the vordpress theme.

1. Go to http://www.hidaia-alassouli.000space.com /wp-admin , and enter using your administrator usename and password

2. Go to appearance, then themes, choose install themes

You can search and test proper theme. I chose to install Gibson. I searched for it, then I installed it after giving the ftp parameters.
   Ftp hostname: ftp.000space.com
   Ftp username: space_15864003

Otherwise, you can download the theme to your computer and upload the zip file to the web hosting using the online file manager to / to http://www.hidaia-alassouli.000space.com/htdocs/wp-content/themes folder
3. Make the Gibson your default theme

v. Creating the frontpage post and the other pages.

1. Go to http://www.hidaia-alassouli.000space.com /wp-admin, and enter using your administrator usename and password
2. Click posts, then add new, and write the necessary information required by your first post, then click publish
3. Go to pages, then add new, and write the necessary information required in your page. I created many pages. You can sort the pages through the order box

vi. Adding Gallery Plugin.
1. Search for suitable Gallery Plugin that can be used. I just found that the Cincopa plugin (Post video players, slideshow albums, photo galleries and music / podcast playlist) is the best for me as it can create image gllaries and add side shows and photo albums
2. Install the Cincopa plugin (Post video players, slideshow albums, photo galleries and music / podcast playlist) either directly or download it from http://wordpress.org/extend/plugins/ website. Then you can upload the zip file using the web hosting online file manager to /.hidaia-alassouli.000space.com/htdocs/wpcontent/plugins folder, Cincopa plugin may request you to install other plugins, so just install them and activate them.
3. After installation, go to Cincopa, then manage Galleries, then create new gallery, and add the necessary photos. Your created gallery will have some id
4. To show the created gallery in your website, in the administrator control panel go to appearance, then choose widgets, then take the Cincopa Gallery Widget to the Sidebar Widget Area, and in the Cincopa Gallery Widget settings enter the ID of your gallery.

vii. Adding Donation Plugin.
1. Go to http://www.hidaia-alassouli.000space.com /wp-admin, then choose plugins, then add new, search for WP Simple Paypal Donation Plugin or Donations Widget or any other suitable donation plugin. I just preferred to use . WP Simple Paypal Donation Plugin. Install it directly. Otherwise download it from http://wordpress.org/extend/plugins/ website. Then you can upload the zip file using the web hosting online file manager to hidaia-alassouli.000space.com /htdocs/wpcontent/plugins folder.
2. In the administrator control panel go to appearance, then choose widgets, then take the WP Simple Paypal Donation Widget to the Sidebar Widget Area. From setting, you can change the options of the WP Simple Paypal Donation and set the email address.

viii. Adding yoast seo plugin and submission the Site to search engine and analyze your website.
1. Search for suitable yoast seo Plugin that can be used. I just tried to add yoast seo plugin. I installed Seo meta tag directly. Otherwise download it from http://wordpress.org/extend/plugins/ website. Then you can upload the zip file using the web hosting online file manager to / hidaia-alassouli.000space.com /htdocs/wpcontent/ plugins folder.
2. Edit each post and each page tags through the custom fields.
3.   To submit the site to websites. There are bulk number of websites that can do submission for you.

ix. Installing Grunion Contact Form Plugin
1- Install **Grunion Contact Form** Plugin.
2- Create contact Page.
3- Add custom form and adjust the email settings.

x. Testing easyfile Ecommerce plugin to sell ebooks.

1. Download easyfile shop from http://wordpress.org/extend/plugins/easyfileshop. Upload easyfileshop folder to the /wp-content/plugins/ directory.
2. Create a folder /wp-content/easyfileshop/ on the server and make it writable (chmod 777 or less). The shop files will be stored in this folder. An .htaccess file will be created automatically.
3. Activate the plugin through the 'Plugins' menu in WordPress.
4. Open the settings page in the new top level 'Easyfileshop' menu.
5. Select a currency and enter your paypal email address.
6. (Opt.) You can select a return/thank you page.
7. Edit or create a Page or Post. Find the paragraph (metabox) Easyfileshop at the bottom of the edit page (admin view). Upload a file and enter a price.
8. Type the short code [easyfileshop] into the content of the post/page.
   Note: I noted there was no download link after completing the payment. So this method not efficient.

xi. Easy digitaleasydownload to sell ebooks

1. Install **Easy Digital Downloads Plugin. You will notice that new pages** for Checkout, Purchase confirmation, purchase history and transec**tion** failed are added.
2. Change the payment gateway to be Paypal. Add the paypal email address.
3. In Misc section, mark Require that users be logged-in to purchase files.
4. In wordpress general setting, mark the membership (anyone can register). Choose New User Default Role to be subscriber.
5. Create new download. My purchase short code was [purchase_link id="250" text="Add to Cart" style="button" color="blue"]
6. Create the page to sell the products. Under the product name of the download created , put the short code, eg:

   - Monitoring of Power System Quality

   - [purchase_link id="250" text="Purchase" style="button" color="blue"]

Note: The Plugin worked fine with me.

xii. WP shopping Plugin

1. Search tor suitable E-commerce Plugin that can be used. I just tried WP Shopping Cart plugin. Install **Using** it directly. Otherwise download it from http://wordpress.org/extend/plugins/ website. Then you can upload the zip file using the web hosting online file manager to htdocs/wpcontent/plugins folder.
2. As the installation is done, we are going to look at the settings of the plugin. Click "WP Shopping Cart" Under Settings. Change the paypal account.
3. Create new page for your product.

- **Step 1)** To add an 'Add to Cart' button for a product simply add the shortcode [wp_cart_button name="PRODUCT-NAME"` price="PRODUCT-PRICE"] to a post or page next to the product. Replace PRODUCT-NAME and PRODUCT-PRICE with the actual name and price of your product.

  Example add to cart button shortcode usage:

  [wp_cart_button name="Reactive Power Compensation " price="30"]

- **Step 2)** To add the shopping cart to a post or page (example: a checkout page) simply add the shortcode [show_wp_shopping_cart] to a post or page or use the sidebar widget to add the shopping cart to the sidebar.

  Example shopping cart shortcode usage:

  [show_wp_shopping_cart]

xiii.   Using Woocommerce to sell ebooks

1. Install Woocommerce Plugin. You will notice that new pages for Shop, Your Account, Cart and Checkout are added. If they were not added, create them as instructed.
2. In woocommerce settings, choose the pages for your account and cart and checkout. Change the payment gateway to be standard Paypal. Add the paypal email address.
3. In woocommerce settings, enable secure login of the user to force the user login when checkout .
4. In wordpress general setting, mark the membership (anyone can register). Choose New User Default Role to be subscriber. Add the metatag widget in the sidebar.
5. Create new product. Add the download file monitoring.docx.
6. The new ebook product will appear in shop page in the menue.
7. When checkout, the user must login before checkout.
8. Organize the menu as you like.
9. To download the file, the downloaded file will be in your account section under your download section.
10. Note: The WP-Ecommerce Plugin worked fine with me.

Note: The Woocommerce Plugin worked fine with me.

Dr. Hidaia Alassouli Personal Website

Home   Curriculum Vitae   Journal and Conference Publications   Sold E-Books   Contact   Stories of Corruptions in My Life

My Arabic Anti-Corruption Website   Shop

Dr. Hidaia Mahmood AlAssouli (د. هدايه محمود العسولي)

Posted on February 12, 2015 by halassouli

Dr. Hidaia Mahmood AlAssouli

(Dr. Hedaya Mahmood Alasooly, د. هدايه محمود العسولي)

I am Dr. Hidaia Alassouli. I completed my PhD degree in Electrical Engineering from Czech Technical University by February 2003, and my M. Sc. degree in n Electrical Engineering from Bahrain University by June 1995. My nationality is Palestinian.

I was appointed in university of Swaziland as lecturer in Electrical Engineering Department since they have no position name Assistant Professor from Jan 2011-Dec 2014. I was teaching Switchgear and Protection, Power Systems, Electrical Machines, Power Electronics, Control Systems, Communication Systems, Fundamentals of Electrical Power Engineering, Introduction of Digital Signal Processing, power operation and control.

c) Part II: Building Ecommerce with mystile and woocommerce plugin:

i. Registering in Free Web Host and Creating Domain

You can see in the web site http://www.absolutely-free-hosting.com/free_hosts_01.php some of the free web hosting. I chose to install my site in the www.000space.com. I created an account in www.000space.com. I created the subdomain http://hedaya-alasooly.000space.com. The following account details are provided

Main Hosting Details		
Control panel username	space_16019985	
Control panel password	**********	
Control panel URL	**cpanel.000space.com**	
MySQL username	space_16019985	
MySQL password	**********	
MySQL hostname	sql303.000space.com	
FTP username	space_16019985	
FTP password	**********	
FTP host name	ftp.000space.com	
Your Website URL's		
Home page	http://hedaya-alasooly.000space.com	

ii. Creating MySQL database

1. Under database management in control panel, choose MySQL database

2. Create database with a name as example sql303.000space.com

iii. Downloading and installing wordpress package

1. Download wordpress 4.1 from http://wordpress.org/download/ site in your desktop.

2. Try to uncompress the zip file, then compress all contents of word press folder in new zip file wordpress.zip

3. In the web hosting control panel under file management, choose online file manager

4. Go to htdocs directory

5. Click upload, then choose to upload Archives (zip, tar, tgz, gz) and upload wordpress.zip

6. Browse again to /hedaya-alasooly.000space.com/htdocs directory, and there will be file wp-config-sample.php, rename the file in the file manager to wp-config.php, and edit the file in the following points:

   // ** MySQL settings - You can get this info from your web host ** //

   /** The name of the database for WordPress */

   define('DB_NAME', ' space_16019985'_wpress');

   /** MySQL database username */

   define('DB_USER', ' space_16019985');

   /** MySQL database password */

   define('DB_PASSWORD', 'main password');

   /** MySQL hostname */

   define('DB_HOST', ' sql303.000space.com');

7. Now in the internet browser go to the website http://www.hedaya-alasooly.000space.com and continue the installation of the wordpress package. Note you will be required the username and password of the administrator. Even if you did not create the wpconfig.php before, the installation process can create it and will ask you the previous mentioned database information in step 5. To administer wordpress, you need to go to http://www.hedaya-alasooly.000space.com/wp-admin

iv. Changing the wordpress theme to mystyle

1. Download Mystile theme from woothemes web site after registration

2. Go to appearance, then themes. Choose new theme and upload Mystyle them and install it, then activate it. Change the settings according to your need.

3. Create about page and **put the necessary information about your store**

4. Install **Grunion Contact Form** Plugin.

5. Create contact Page. Add custom form and adjust the email settings.

v. **Installing woocommerce plugin**

1. From plugin, search excelling woocommerce plugin and install it. Change the settings accoding to your need and put your paypal setting.

2. There will be many pages creates: Shop. Checkout, Cart, My Account.

3. Create new top menu and include on it About and contact us and home pages.

4. Create new main menue and include on it Shop. Checkout, Cart, My Account and product categories pages

5. Change the paypal setting and other settings of woocommerce as you prefer

vi. **Adding woocommerce producrs**

1. Create woocommerce new product. Assign the category of each product created. For example, E-Books category for the Ebooks

2. Any new product will occur in the shop page automatically.

3. The recent products will be appearing in home page.

4. Note that I tried the woocommerce and it was working fine.

Mail - hidaia_alassouli@hotma... × | Content Creation Wizard × | الرئيسية : موقع مكافحة الفساد — ووردبرس × | Dr. Hedaya Alasooly Ecommerce × | ⚠ Insecure Connection × |

← → C ⌂   ⓘ www.hedaya-alasooly.000space.com   ⋯ ✓ ☆

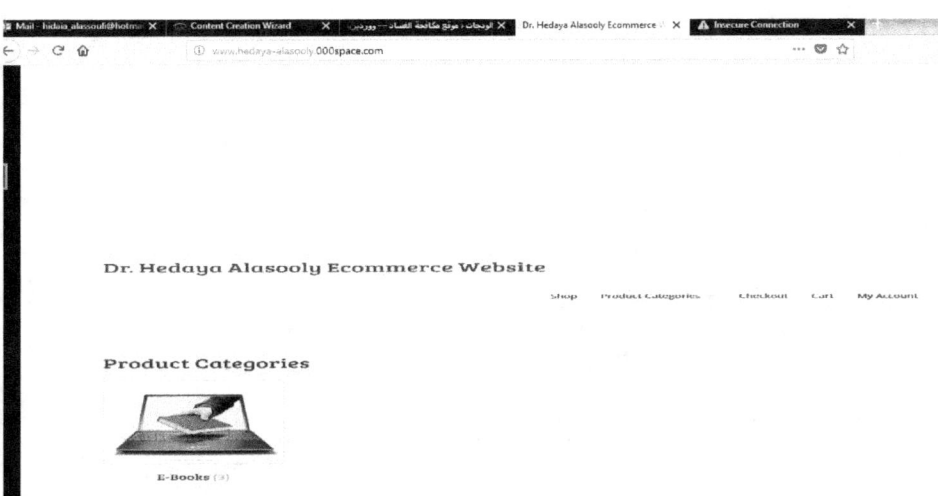

Dr. Hedaya Alasooly Ecommerce Website

Shop   Product Categories   Checkout   Cart   My Account

Product Categories

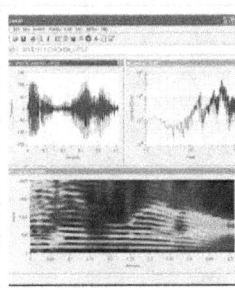

E-Books (3)

Recent Products

⌂   ⓘ www.hedaya-alasooly.000space.com

Recent Products

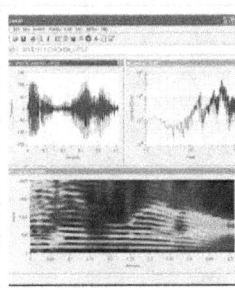

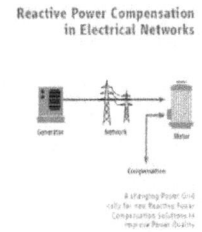

Signal, Audio and Image Processing	Reactive Power Compensation	Monitoring of Power System Quality
$32.00	$30.00	$0.05

13

Shop   Product Categories   Checkout   Cart   My Account

E-Books

Showing all 3 results   Default sorting ▾

 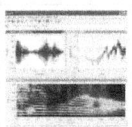

Monitoring of   Reactive Power   Signal, Audio and

Monitoring of Power System Quality

$0.05

This project will tackle the subject of Power Quality, Power Quality Disturbances, Power Quality Standards as well as Power Quality Monitoring. A general description of each of the disturbances will be given, and the basic techniques which are used to mitigate that disturbance so as to improve the quality of the supply are presented.

1 ⌖   Add to cart

Category: E-Books

14

d) Building Online Magazine With MH Magazine Theme:

i. Registering in Free Web Host and Creating Domain

You can see in the web site http://www.absolutely-free-hosting.com/free_hosts_01.php some of the free web hosting. I chose to install my site in the www.000space.com

I created an account in www.000space.com. I created the subdomain http://anticorruption.000space.com. The following account details are provided

```
⊞ Main Web Hosting¶
    Cpanel Username:········space_16115534↵
    Cpanel Password:·······godhed321↵
    Your URL:············http://anticorruption.000space.com· or·
    http://www.anticorruption.000space.com↵
    FTP Server··········ftp.000space.com↵
    FTP Login·········space_16115534↵
    FTP Password:········godhed321↵
    MySQL Database Name:····MUST CREATE IN CPANEL↵
    MySQL Username·········space_16115534↵
    MySQL Password·········godhed321↵
    MySQL Server:········SEE THE CPANEL¶
    Cpanel URL:···········http://cpanel.000space.com/¶
```

ii. Creating MySqL database
1. Under database management in control panel, choose MySQL database
2. Create database with a name as example space_16115534_wpress

iii. Downloading and Installing wordpress packages:

1. Download wordpress 4.1 from http://wordpress.org/download/ site in your desktop.
2. **Testing easyfile Ecommerce plugin to sell ebooks.**
3. Try to uncompress the zip file, then compress all contents of word press folder in new zip file wordpress.zip
4. In the web hosting control panel under file management, choose online file manager.
5. Go to htdocs directory
6. Click upload, then choose to upload Archives (zip, tar, tgz, gz) and upload wordpress.zip
7. Browse again to /anticorreption.000space.com/htdocs directory, and there will be file wp-config-sample.php, rename the file in the file manager to wp-config.php, and edit the file in the following points:
   // ** MySQL settings - You can get this info from your web host ** //
   /** The name of the database for WordPress */
   define('DB_NAME', ' space_16115534_wpress');
   /** MySQL database username */

```
define('DB_USER',' space_16115534');
/** MySQL database password */
define('DB_PASSWORD', 'main password');
/** MySQL hostname */
define('DB_HOST', ' sql309.000space.com');
```

8. Now in the internet browser go to the website http://www.anticorruption.com and continue the installation of the wordpress package. Note you will be required the username and password of the administrator. Even if you did not create the wpconfig.php before, the installation process can create it and will ask you the previous mentioned database information in step 5. To administer wordpress, you need to go to http://www.anticorruption.000space.com /wp-admin

iv. Downloading and Installing wordpress packages:

1. Download wordpress 4.1 from http://wordpress.org/download/ site in your desktop.
2. **Testing** easyfile **Ecommerce plugin to sell ebooks.**
3. Try to uncompress the zip file, then compress all contents of word press folder in new zip file wordpress.zip
4. In the web hosting control panel under file management, choose online file manager.
5. Go to htdocs directory
6. Click upload, then choose to upload Archives (zip, tar, tgz, gz) and upload wordpress.zip
7. Browse again to /anticorreption.000space.com/htdocs directory, and there will be file wp-config-sample.php, rename the file in the file manager to wp-config.php, and edit the file in the following points:
   ```
   // ** MySQL settings - You can get this info from your web host ** //
   /** The name of the database for WordPress */
   define('DB_NAME', ' space_16115534_wpress');
   /** MySQL database username */
   define('DB_USER',' space_16115534');
   /** MySQL database password */
   define('DB_PASSWORD', 'main password');
   /** MySQL hostname */
   define('DB_HOST', ' sql309.000space.com');
   ```

8. Now in the internet browser go to the website http://www.anticorruption.com and continue the installation of the wordpress package. Note you will be required the username and password of the administrator. Even if you did not create the wpconfig.php before, the installation process can create it and will ask you the previous mentioned database information in step 5. To administer wordpress, you need to go to http://www.anticorruption.000space.com /wp-admin

v. Downloading and Installing and Configuring MH magazine theme:

1. Download the MH magazine premium theme from www.4shared.com
2. When you have activated the *MH Magazine* theme, then it will list your posts chronological by default. To create a magazine style front page, you will have to use the fully widgetized homepage template. In order to do this, you need to create a new page and select **"Homepage"** as template for your page. When

you have created and published your page, then you need to set this page as your static front page in your WordPress dashboard at **"Settings => Reading"**.

3. Widgets: *MH Magazine* theme has in total 25 locations where you can place WordPress widgets, custom widgets or add any HTML code you like. *MH Magazine* comes with 6 custom widgets: Slider Widget, Spotlight Widget, Custom Posts Widget, Carousel Widget, Custom Pages Widget and News in Pictures Widget. In the following, please see what these custom widgets can do.

- **Slider Widget**: This widget displays large featured images with title and excerpt (optional). The Slider Widget is preferred to be used in widget area *"Home 1"* on the homepage template. You can select one category or all categories to be displayed; and you are able to filter multiple categories by ID or filter posts by tags. You may determine the post number, skip posts and choose the post order (latest, random, popular). Depending on the selected widget location for the Slider Widget, you can adapt the image size (940 x 400px or 620 x 264px). Regarding the excerpt, you are free to adapt the excerpt length or disable the excerpt entirely. For this to work, you need a featured image set.

- **Spotlight Widget:** You may use the Spotlight Widget to present special posts in a prominent position. This widget is best to be utilized in the widget area *"Home 2"* on the homepage template. You may enter a title and you can choose a single category or all categories to be displayed; besides you can filter posts by tags. You can show latest, random or popular posts and skip posts if you like. Depending on the widget location you choose for the Spotlight Widget, you have two options regarding the image size (940 x 400px or 580 x 326px). Further you may determine the excerpt length and disable the excerpt, post meta or comments.

- **Custom Posts Widget:** The Custom Posts Widget can be used to display posts based on categories or tags. This widget shows thumbnails and excerpts below each other. Therefore you can select the post number and also skip posts. Besides, you are able to show latest, random or popular posts. Regarding the excerpts, you can determine their lengths and display excerpts for all posts, the first post or show no excerpts at all. Show / hide all thumbnails or just select the small / large thumbnails to be shown / hidden. Further, you can hide the date or the comment count.

- **Carousel Widget**: This widget shows an arbitrary number of thumbnails which are linked to the content and rotate as you click the arrow. The Carousel Widget is preferred to be used in widget area *"Home 7"* on your homepage template. You may either choose a certain category to be shown, all categories or you can filter multiple categories by ID. Besides, you may select the post order (latest posts, random posts or popular posts). The Carousel Widget offers two types of layouts and you can also display a title if you wish.

- **Custom Pages Widget:** With this widget you can display pages based on page IDs. This widget shows the page title, thumbnails and an excerpt. You may show a title and link it to a URL – both is optional. If you like, you can show an excerpt for the first page, all pages or no excerpts at all. Displaying an excerpt you may limit the characters as you prefer. Regarding the thumbnails, you may display / hide all thumbnails or display / hide all large / small thumbnails.

- **News in Pictures Widget:** This widget shows a square shaped gallery of small thumbnails which are linked to the post content. You may display all categories or a certain category; and you can filter multiple categories by ID or filter posts by tags. Further, you can choose an arbitrary number of thumbnails to be displayed and you may determine to display latest, random or popular posts.

4. Remove default widgets from Header: When you activate the *MH Magazine* theme for the first time, then you might have some default WordPress widgets in your header. To remove these widgets, please navigate to **"Appearance => Widgets"** in your WordPress dashboard and just remove the widgets from the **"Header"** widget location.

5. Available Widget Locations: These are the available widget locations in the *MH Magazine* theme:

   - **Header:** widget area above the logo

   - **Sidebar:** widget area located in your sidebar

   - **Sidebar 2:** second sidebar (has to be activated in the theme options)

   - **Home 1 – Home 11:** widget areas on "Homepage" template

   - **Home 12:** sidebar on homepage template (only active when site width is 1300px)

   - **Posts 1:** widget area above post content

   - **Posts 2:** widget area below post content

   - **Pages 1:** widget area above page content

   - **Pages 2:** widget area below page content

   - **Footer 1 – Footer 4:** widget areas located in footer

   - **Contact:** widget area on contact page template

   - **Contact 2:** second sidebar on contact page (has to be activated in the theme options)

6. Widget location **"Home 12″** will be only available if you have activated it in the built-in layout options. If you want to increase the width of your site, then please navigate to **"Appearance => Customize => Layout Options"** in your WordPress dashboard and set the site width to 1300px. When you have saved this setting, the widget location **"Home 12″** will be available.

MH Magazine theme uses featured images for all thumbnails. It is recommended to upload images with a size of at least **940 x 400px** (especially when you are using the large slider). In that case all required thumbnails will be generated automatically by WordPress

vi.   Creating the front page like the theme demo:

1. After you have completed the setup of your static front page, you can easily *drag&drop* widgets in the **"Home 1″** until **"Home 12″** widget areas and they will be displayed on the homepage template. If you want to create the same layout as used in the theme demo, please check the widget map below. There you can see the locations of the widget areas on the fully widgetized homepage template. Now you can follow this list and add the widgets to the specific widget locations to have the same layout as in the demo:

   - **Home 1:** Slider Widget
   - **Home 2:** Spotlight Widget
   - **Home 6:** Custom Posts Widget
   - **Home 7:** Carousel Widget
   - **Home 8 – Home 10:** 2 x Custom Posts Widget
   - **Footer 1:** News in Pictures Widget
   - **Footer 2:** Custom Posts Widget
   - **Footer 3:** Custom Posts Widget
   - **Footer 4:** Textwidget

2. **Custom Menus:** *MH Magazine* theme supports custom menus with multi-level dropdown support. If you don't know how you can create custom menus in WordPress, then please check this tutorial: Custom Menus. The theme has included 4 custom menu slots:

   - Header
   - Main Navigation
   - Infomenu below Main Navigation
   - Footer

3. **New Tickers:** *MH Magazine* comes with a sleek little news ticker for your posts. Here you can filter posts by categories or tags to display breaking news, announcements or just any other kind of posts you like. You can enable the news ticker in your WordPress dashboard under **"Appearance => Customize => News Ticker Options"**.

4. **Images:** *MH Magazine* theme uses featured images for all thumbnails. It is recommended to upload images with a size of at least **940 x 400px** (especially when you are using the large slider). In that case all required thumbnails will be generated automatically by WordPress

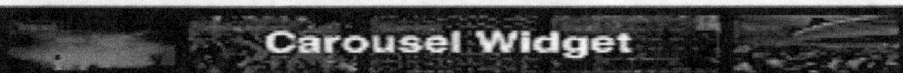

موقع مكافحة الفساد
موقع مكافحة الفساد الفلسطيني والاسرائيلي والعالمي

الصفحة الرئيسيه | الارشيف | ردود القراء | اتصل بنا | فساد الجامعات | فساد المؤسسات الصحيه | فساد مؤسسات هندسة الكهرباء بالقطاع | الفساد الاسرائيلي | فساد الفصال

فساد الدول العربيه والغربيه | فساد الانترنت | فساد مؤسسات السلطة الفلسطينيه | فساد اجتماعي

News Ticker | أزمة مقتعلة لوقود المشافي

المصالحه في غرفة الانعاش
[...]

فساد الجامعات

احدث المقالات

احدث المقالات

أزمة مقتعله لوقود المشافي
Comments 0

تعيب على احدث المنجمات: صفقة القرن وزياره البروفسور عنان مجلس القطاع:
Comments 0

هل سينا مصريه أم فلسطينيه ؟؟

المواطن الغزاوي بين مطرقة الانتعاش الكهربائي وسنديان الملاحقة القانونية مع تطبيق براءة الذمه
Comments 0

قراءة لاهم ما ورد في خطاب الرئيس الفلسطيني في اجتماع المجلس المركزي لمنظمه التحرير الفلسطيني.
Comments 0

اهم الفوارق بين البنوك التي تعاملت بها في فلسطين
Comments 0

ما بين ماجد حجي وعماد حجي .. اين الحقيقه

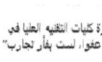

الي ادارة الكليات العليا للتقنيه في الامارات .. لن ينصر عجزيتكم قاصر ولا وكيل نيابه، فهم ليسوا باجورين

من استاذه جامعيه لادارة كليات التقنيه العليا في الامارات: "وماذا بعد.. عفوا، لست بفأر لتجارب"
Comments 0

فساد اكاديمي في كليات التقنيه العليا للطالبات ببي
Comments 0

من فضائح الجامعات الخاصه خارج فلسطين
Comments 0

تعليبا على الدكتور كمال الشرافي من السفر
Comments 0

فساد الجامعات

من استاذه اكاديميه الي الكليات العليا للتقنيه في الامارات:" اني بريئه من درجاتكم التي تغشون"
Comments 0

كليات التقنيه العليا في الامارات .. مشروع استقطاب الكوادر الاكاديميه بهدف تدميرها
Comments 0

استاذه اكاديميه مصريه تم موقوفه عن العمل في كليات التقنيه العليا للطالبات ببي .. كفاكم تخبطا
Comments 0

مخالصه او مراوغه مع الكليات العليا للتقنيه للطالبات في بي
Comments 0

بين تصريحات د كمال الشرافي والدكتور زياد ثابت بخصوص جامعة الاقصى
Comments 0

ARAB BANK

الفساد الاسرائيلي

قراءة لاهم ما ورد في خطاب الرئيس الفلسطيني في

فساد المؤسسات الصحيه

هل يوجد قرار بعدم اعطاء الفلسطيني في مصر

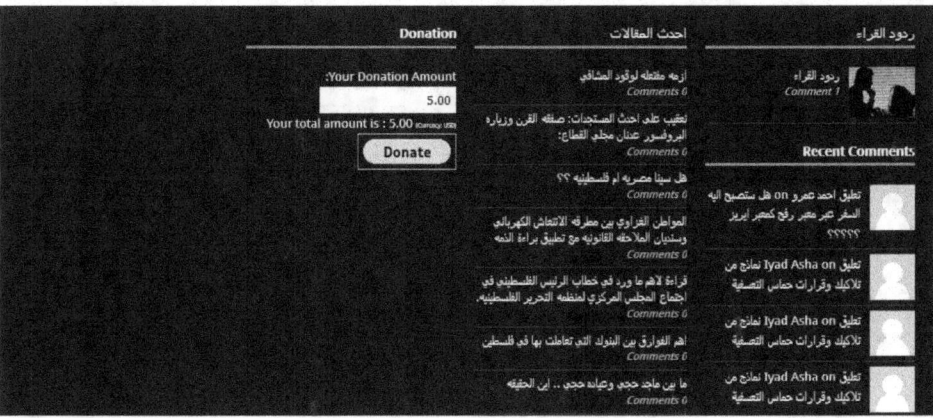

كتاب مشرف لاستقاله الوزير السابق شوقي العبـه.

Donation	احدث المقالات	ردود القراء
:Your Donation Amount	ازمه مقطعه لوقود المشافي	ردود القراء
5.00		Comment 1
Your total amount is : 5.00 (Currency USD)	تعيب على احدث المستجدات: صفقه القرن وزياره البروفسور عدنان مطلو القطاع:	
Donate	Comments 0	**Recent Comments**
	هل سينا مصريه ام فلسطينيه ؟؟	
	Comments 0	تطبيق احمد عمرو on هل ستصبح اليه السفر عبر معبر رفح كمعبر ايريز
	المواطن الغزاوي بين مطرقه الانتعاش الكهربائي	؟؟؟؟؟
	وستنيان العلاقه القانونيه مع تطبيق براءة الذمه	
	Comments 0	تطبيق Iyad Asha on نمازج من
	قراءة لاهم ما ورد في خطاب الرئيس الفلسطيني في	تلاكيك وقرارات حماس التصفية
	اجتماع المجلس المركزي لمنظمه التحرير الفلسطينيه	
	Comments 0	تطبيق Iyad Asha on نمازج من
	اهم الفوارق بين البنود التي تعاملت بها في فلسطين	تلاكيك وقرارات حماس التصفية
	Comments 0	تطبيق Iyad Asha on نمازج من
	ما بين ماجد حجي وعياده حجي .. اين الحقيقه	تلاكيك وقرارات حماس التصفية
	Comments 0	

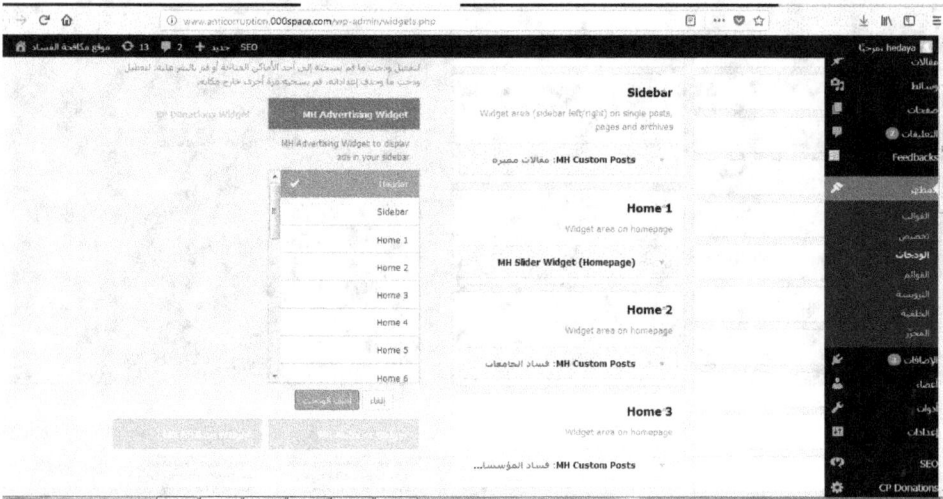

السخة 3.0.4 | بواسطة Automattic | عرض التفاصيل.

⊕هناك نسخة جديدة من أكيسميت. مشاهدة تفاصيل النسخة 4.0.2 أو التحديث الآن.

This WordPress plugin will allow you to create unique customized PayPal donation widgets on WordPress posts or pages and accept donations. Creates custom PayPal donation widgets.

Custom Post Donations
تعطيل تحرير

السخة 4.1 | بواسطة HahnCreativeGroup | عرض التفاصيل | Donate

⊕هناك نسخة جديدة من Custom Post Donations. مشاهدة تفاصيل النسخة 4.2.1 أو التحديث الآن.

Add a contact form to any post, page or text widget. Emails will be sent to the post's author by default, or any email address you choose. As seen on WordPress.com.

Grunion Contact Form
تعطيل تحرير

السخة 2.3 | بواسطة Automattic, Inc | زيارة موقع الإضافة.

هالو دولي (بالإنجليزية: Hello, Dolly!) هي موسيقى من تأليف الملحن الأمريكي جيري هيرمان وأشهر من عناها كان لويس أرمسترونج. بالنسبة لمؤسسي وورديريس، تعتبر هذه الأغنية رمزاً للأمل والحماس لذلك نجدوها مُدمجة مع إصدارات وورديريس. عند تفعيل الإضافة سيتم عرض عبارات عشوائية من هذه الأغنية في الطرف العلوي الأيسر من الشاشة.

هالو دولى
تعطيل تحرير حذف

السخة 1.6 | بواسطة Matt Mullenweg | عرض التفاصيل.

The first true all-in-one SEO solution for WordPress, including on-page content analysis, XML sitemaps and much more.

WordPress SEO
FAQ مدفوع إعدادات تعطيل تحرير

السخة 2.1.1 | بواسطة Team Yoast | عرض التفاصيل.

Add a simple PayPal button of custom buttons to any widget place on your wordpress blog and accept donations or payments from your users.

WP Paypal Simple Donation Widget
تعطيل تحرير

السخة 1.5.1 | بواسطة Jack Ripping | عرض التفاصيل

www.ingramcontent.com/pod-product-compliance
Lightning Source LLC
Chambersburg PA
CBHW071205220526
45468CB00003B/1161